By His Stripes We are Healed

He Healed Me Twice from Cancer,
Without Medication

How You Can Be Healed From Cancer
or Any Other Disease

Cheryl D. Forrest

Copyright © 2010 by Cheryl Forrest

By His Stripes We are Healed
He Healed Me Twice From Cancer, Without Medication
by Cheryl Forrest

Printed in the United States of America

ISBN 9781609578909

All rights reserved solely by the author. The author guarantees all contents are original and do not infringe upon the legal rights of any other person or work. No part of this book may be reproduced in any form without the permission of the author. The views expressed in this book are not necessarily those of the publisher.

Unless otherwise indicated, Bible quotations are taken from The New King James Version of the Bible. Copyright © 1997 by Thomas Nelson, Inc.

www.xulonpress.com

Dedication

This book is first dedicated to my Heavenly Father, for if it had not been for Divine intervention in my life, I would not be here today to tell of His goodness.

To my wonderful husband, Apostle Steven A. Forrest, Sr., for his love, prayers, encouragement, help and support.

To my four sons, Willie Cunningham, Jr., Anthony Cunningham, Michael Cunningham and Steven Forrest Jr., for their love and the many sacrifices they made for the sake of the Ministry.

To my precious grandchild, Chloe, whose beautiful smile fills my life with great joy.

I love you all.

Table of Contents

Introduction ix
Chapter 1. A Supernatural Covenant 15
Chapter 2. Use the Right Keys 21
Chapter 3. The Keys of Doubt, Unbelief and Fear 23
Chapter 4. The Power of Expectation 25
Chapter 5. There is a Way that Seems Right 29
Chapter 6. God wants to Heal You 32
Chapter 7. God Dissolves Lumps and Growths 36
Chapter 8. Whose Report will you Believe 42
Chapter 9. Our Provision is Wrapped up in Our
    Obedience 49
Chapter 10. The Paralyzing Affects of Unforgiveness 54
Chapter 11. Healing Scriptures 57
Chapter 12 Healings in the Bible 63
Conclusion 73

Table of Contents

Introduction

Over the years, I've been the beneficiary of several personal healings, and miracles in my own life. I've personally experienced God as Jehovah Rapha the Lord God our healer.

God has healed me from cancer twice, without medication, losing my hair or changing my diet. He dissolved a lump that was on my breast, healed me from fibroids, infections, reoccurring styes on my eyelids, back problems and much more.

As a young child, approximately four or five years old, I ran out from between two parked cars into the street; I was hit by a car, and walked away alive and well.

God has blessed me to pray for many that have been healed, physically, emotionally and spiritually from: deafness, M.S., cancer, back problems, infertility, lumps, pains, growths, fibroids, injuries and much more.

This book shares testimonies of the healing power of God, and the steps and acts of obedience we followed to receive our healings. God loves us, and He has made the necessary provisions for us to receive our healing.

Within the pages of this book, you will find guidance and help to receive your healing.

God is a very present help in times of trouble. He is real, and He's healing and working miracles today. The same anointing to heal the sick when Jesus walked the earth is available to heal you today.

Jesus answered and said to them, "have faith in God. For assuredly, I say to you, whoever says to this Mountain "Be removed and be cast into the sea," and does not doubt in his heart, but believes that those things he says will be done, he will have whatever he says. Therefore I say to you, whatever things you ask when you pray, believe that you receive them, and you will have them. Mark 11:22-24 NKJV

Ask, and it will be given to you;
seek, and you will find;
knock, and it will be opened to you.
For everyone who asks receives,
and he who seeks finds,
and to him who knocks it will be opened.
Matthews 7:7-8 NKJV

Is there anything or any sickness, aliment, ache or pain to hard for God?
No! There's no limit to the ability of Gods power to answer prayer or to heal a sick body.

A Supernatural Covenant

It was never God's intent that man would be anything less than victorious, mighty, healed, delivered and well. Contrary to belief, sickness and premature death is not God's best for us. Life and that more abundantly is the lot in life God prepared for us from the beginning.

Through satanic influences over the years, man lost his victory in the garden, but because of the sacrifice of innocent blood shed at Calvary by Jesus, we were reinstated to receive the rites to inherit the promises of God.

Healing is part of a supernatural covenant that God initiated with our forefathers.

If you walk in my statutes and keep my commandments, and perform them, I will look on you favorably and make you fruitful, multiply you and confirm My covenant with you. Lev. 26:3,9

His word indicates that we should adopt a lifestyle of walking by faith and not by sight. It is our faith that causes God our Creator to move on our behalf. The Word specifically tells us; in order to please Him we must have faith. God, in His slender, lessens our portion of faith to that of a grain of mustard seed to be sufficient enough to move mountains. As the body of Christ, we must gravitate to the fact that in order to live a victorious life, we must have faith and be willing to use the faith we possess to overpower negative circumstances that arise in our life.

Faith without works is dead; therefore we must use our faith by putting it in action. If a little faith can move a mountain, then much faith can bring about great victories.

While walking through the house one day, I bumped my leg against a sharp object. The pain was intense and throbbing, I felt like going to the hospital. I reached down and touched the injured area, hoping to bring comfort by rubbing it and repeatedly calling on the name of Jesus. By now I'm hopping, limping, trying to reach the sofa and wanting to cry. My son Steven Jr., (who had not started elementary school) saw me in pain, said a short prayer, look at me and said, "Now walk!" The Holy Spirit quickened me, if I ignored my son and continued to nurse my pain, it could hinder his spiritual growth and faith in God. I knew I had a choice to make, so I stepped out on faith and began to walk normal. The pain was completely gone. I was healed. What the devil meant for bad, God turned it around and gave me the victory. Glory to God!

God is able to do exceedingly, abundantly, above all that we ask or think. It's God ability empowered by faith that will cause mountains to be moved on our behalf. Not our ability not our wisdom but His.

We must trust Him regardless of what it feels like. It has been proven in the Word of God, that God is "I Am." From the very beginning of history until this very day, God is still working miracles. He is still healing His people and as always, He's the chief door opener.

Once a week, I'm privileged to teach bible study at a location outside of our church. A couple came in one evening that had received an invitation on facebook to join us. While waiting to start, I began to share my testimony with them of how God supernaturally healed me twice from cancer without medication. They listened intensely. Before the actual teaching, we began to praise and worship God until His presence filled the room. After the Bible Study was over the wife, who's also a minister from another church, asked me to look at her; she had her arm raised up above her head. She began to testify that she'd had surgery, and for months she was unable to lift her arm up in this position. She also shared with us that for months she was unable to sleep in her bed at night. We began to rejoice and praise God for her healing. God is so amazing! Now she could go home and sleep in her own bed without pain.

God is not slack concerning his promises, whatever He promised He has the ability and power to bring it to pass. God wants us healed and God wants us whole.

After healing the woman (in Matthews 9:20) with the issue of blood for twelve years, He gave her more then what she expected. She said within herself, "If I could just touch the hem of His garment I will be made whole," and her faith pushed her to realizing or receiving her desire. Jesus asked, "who touched Me," because this wasn't and ordinary touch; this was a touch of faith that was extended to the Bread of Life: Christ the Anointed One.

Out of Him flows healing, deliverance, salvation, peace, joy, unconditional love, restoration and much more. To be made whole means receiving healing, restoration and whatever we're lacking from the well within Him. God wants us whole in every area of our life: spiritually, physically, emotionally and financially. Faith is the key to unlocking the doors.

Trusting God, means not putting confidence in our own flesh, but in Him.

Mark 11:22 says, *"Have faith in God."* Trusting God might not seem easy or comfortable at first; Especially if we're used to doing everything for ourselves or trusting other people in time of need.

I once had a friend that struggled in the area of faith; we both went through similar trials with threats of losing property and receiving negative reports from doctors. I testified about the importance of walking by faith, but my friend never seemed to conform to faith, instead of fear. Faith in God kept me in my house and has kept me alive to testify about it today. Unfortunately my friend lost her home and died prematurely.

God has a best for us, it's called, *"Beloved I wish above all things that thou may prosper, be in health even as your soul prosper."* God has even promised us houses that we didn't build and vineyards that we did not plant; not to mention, favor to compass us like a shield and the promise to be our helper, provider and healer.

It's time to believe the Word. It's time to trust God. *Trust in the Lord with all your heart, and lean not on your own understanding. In all your ways acknowledge Him, and He shall direct your paths. Prov. 3:5-6*

Use the Right Keys

Doors of opportunity, success and longevity are awaiting our key of faith. God has already put the ball in our court; He's given every one a measure of faith; now it's up to us to use faith as an advantage to open doors in our lives.

The keys of faith will get doors open that will bring about much success, healing, deliverance, and victory in our lives. Our hope will be renewed and the joy of the Lord will be our strength.

If we use the key of faith, it can unlock the doors to every covenant promise in The Word of God. Jesus told his disciples, *"If you have faith as a mustard seed, you will say to this mountain, Move from here to there; and it will move, and nothing will be impossible for you. Matt. 11:22."*

Hebrews defines faith as the substance of things hoped for, the evidence of things not seen. Webster defines faith as unquestioning belief in God. Complete trust or confidence; loyalty.

By faith, the bible says in Hebrews 11th chapter, *Sarah herself also received strength to conceive seed, and she bore a child when she was past the age, because she judged Him faithful who had promised. Therefore from one man, and him as good as dead, were born as many as the stars of the sky in multitude-innumerable as the sand, which is by the seashore.* Faith is not limited to moving mountains. Faith can generate a lifetime of blessed, prosperous days that exceed our expectations. Our decision to trust God has great benefits that can affect generations to come.

A young mother brought her daughter to our church who had been diagnosis by the doctor, with a learning problem and she was unable to walk. Before they left church that day we prayed for God to heal her.

A few weeks later they came back, to join us for another service. While my husband, was preaching he paused, the little girl came out into the aisle and started walking around holding onto the pews. Glory to God! God did it again. Not only did God heal her body so she could walk, He also healed her from the learning disability. She's in school now doing quite well.

The keys of doubt, unbelief and fear

God has not given us a spirit of fear, but of love, power and a sound mind. 2Tim. 1:7

Make sure you're using the right keys. Doubt, unbelief and fear: these keys are a hazard to our health and serious blessing blockers. They have robbed Christians of there victory and caused many to live beneath their means. They have stunted spiritual growth, bolted doors of opportunity, repelled increase, shipwrecked promotions and caused premature death. Doubt, unbelief and fear kept the Israelites out of the promise land with a fate of wandering in the wilderness for forty years with many fatalities.

There are some physical keys in my possession from my past that if I were to use today at liberty would bring heartache, confusion and much regret. So I choose not to use them, but to discard them. The choice is ours; we can experience life and that more abundantly by using the key of faith or sickness, poverty and premature death by living a life of doubt, unbelief and fear.

During one of our Sunday Worship Services at New Creation Ministries, God gave me a prophecy for a woman that had came in with the aid of a walker; she was diagnosed with M.S. He told me to tell her that today was her day for a miracle. We laid hands on her back, and began to pray the prayer of faith. After the prayer the woman moved into the aisle and began to walk without her walker. God is so amazing. We were invited into a miracle as we witnessed Him supernaturally heal her of M.S. *Faith without works is dead. (James 2:20)* She left our Church Service that day healed and helping one of our mature life members walk out the door. She later moved to another state to be with her mother and started her own cleaning business. To God be the glory.

The Power of Expectation

F*or all things are possible to him that believe.*
Two blind men followed Jesus, crying out and saying, Son of David, have mercy on us!"

And when He had come into the house, the blind men came to Him. And Jesus said to them, "Do you believe that I am able to do this?" They said to Him, "Yes, Lord."

Then He touched their eyes, saying, "According to your faith let it be to you." and their eyes were opened. Matt. 9:28

Faith plays a vital part in receiving our healing. This is where we change as people from normalcy to radical in our thinking. The two blind men received their healing because they simply believed. In order to experience the same results, (healed) there must be a yes Lord, I believe mindset within us. We must believe that, "God is able," without traces of doubt and unbelief to pollute our results.

One Sunday after church I went to the hospital to pray for the sick. I knocked on a door and was asked to come in. After introducing myself to the patient I shared my testimony with him of how God healed me of cancer at age 17 and how if he had faith the size of a mustard seed God would heal him. We prayed together, he thanked me for coming and I proceeded to the next room. A few months later I discovered that the man I prayed for was my mothers neighbor; He told her that after the prayer they took him for x-rays the next morning and they couldn't find anything wrong with him. Praise the Lord.

A few years ago, God blessed me to go on a mission's trip to Kampala,Uganda to preach Women's Conferences, a Pastors Conference for pastors wife and female pastors only, and at the end of my trip, an explosive Youth Conference. I was blessed to be apart of an awesome move of God during my stay. After one of the Evening Services, we were given the opportunity to pray for the sick. There were many people lined up for prayer and in need of a miracle from God. At the end of the Service the pastor asked for all that had been healed to come forward and testify. There were numerous testimonies stating that when I prayed for them, God healed them. All of the testimonies were powerful and I give God all the glory. I remember a young girl standing before the congregation with the microphone in her hand; she testified that she was deaf and when I prayed for her, God opened up her ears. I was expecting God to heal His people, and that night He did exceedingly, abundantly more.

One touch from God can change the quality of your life forever.

It can take you from: hopeless to victorious, blind to seeing, deaf to hearing, lame to walking and from infirmed to healed.

I invited a friend to one of our Sunday Worship Services, and she brought a couple along with her that were first time visitors to our church. During the altar call, the Holy Spirit prompted me to tell the people that whatever they needed just ask God for it. The couple had a son at home that couldn't walk so we prayed for God to heal him. A few hours after church I received a phone call. The same friend that attended our church service was very excited. With great joy, she told me when they returned home they discovered that God had miraculously healed their son, he was walking. Praise God! To God be the glory.

Expectation births forth miracles. God desires to work a miracle on your behalf. He wants you healed. Expect your miracle today! Expect your healing today! God can - God will - God wants to heal you!

There is a way that seems right

It's necessary for me to share a little of my past that you might know the depth of the love that God extended to me. At age seventeen the road I traveled was reckless and irresponsible. I wasn't saved, just following the cravings of my flesh smoking, drinking and partying. I truly was deceived. I fell for the lie that everybody was doing it and because I desperately wanted to be accepted I joined in. I soon found out that joining the wrong crowd and partying couldn't make or keep me happy. I was caught up in a lot of stuff, but there was still a void within me. No matter how often I gave into my cravings, I just couldn't shake that empty feeling. It was like something was missing and no matter what I did, it was still there. Sometimes I just felt awkward, like I just didn't fit in.

No God- no peace- no direction.

Know God- know peace- He gives direction.

Six months to once a year doctors appointments became part of the norm for the lifestyle I was living. And according to my Doctors Appointment Card it was time for my yearly check up. The appointment was pretty much routine nothing different. The Same Doctor and the same type of exam. A few days later I received a call from the Doctors Office, they requested a return visit as soon as possible.

At this time in my life my largest concerns were, keeping up with my boyfriend, and preparing for High school graduation.

Dr. Ashby had been my family doctor for as long as I could remember, even as a little girl. I returned to the doctor's office not knowing what to expect. My mindset was whatever it was; he'd probably give me a prescription for medicine with a horrible after taste.

To my surprise, this office visit was much different. Instead of a short talk with the doctor, a prescription in my hand, and out the front door, this time I was given an unexpected diagnosis. Dr. Ashby discloses to me that my Pap smear exam returned abnormal, and after a second examination I was told it was cancer.

I didn't quite know how to take the results of the exams. It wasn't easy being seventeen and having to face the many pressures of keeping up with the crowd. As well as trying to find happiness and true love in an unstable environment.

Just seventeen, at the beginning of my partying years and cancer wasn't the type of report I expected to hear from anyone, especially my doctor concerning me. It was easier to think that I was immune from sicknesses such as this one. Wait a minute, did I fail to mention that I was just 17 years old. This was not included on my list of things I wanted to do, nor the lifestyle I envisioned for my future. There is a way that seems right to a man, but its end is a way of death.

One might think after a report like cancer, my lifestyle would drastically change for the better. Maybe a commitment to doing good deeds for others, at least eating and living healthier. Unfortunately the condition of my heart didn't change, neither was my mindset affected for a lengthy period of time. The truth is, my childhood was so messed up, and I became use to abnormal. So life went on as usual. *The thief comes not but to steal, kill and destroy, but I come that you may have life and that more abundantly. John 10:10*

God Wants to Heal You

I truly thank God for His mercy, His grace and for the prayers that bomb barded heaven on my behalf, from birth till now.

As a teenager I was very rebellious and coming home the next day without prior permission from mom was one of my bad habits. After spending the night out, I came home to discover we had company, my Uncle Robert stop by for a visit (Destiny). My mom had told him about my negative doctors report.

My Uncle Robert was a preacher. It was something different about him. He was the type of preacher that didn't indulge in alcohol or partying with us. When he visited our home we put away all alcohol beverages and smoking was out of the question. We respected him because of his lifestyle and what he represented - Holiness and God.

After greeting him, he looked at me and said, "Cheryl God loves you, and you are to young to die from cancer. God wants to heal you, and if you just have faith the size of a grain of mustard seed, God will heal you from cancer." I jokingly said, "I don't want to die either."

My uncle asked if he could pray for me and I said yes. He said, " Just believe" and he prayed. To be totally honest I believed because my uncle the late Rev. Robert Hicks believed. Even though I wasn't saved, Jesus wasn't Lord of my life and at that time I was not living for Him. I knew my uncle was a righteous man and I trusted the God in him. He that receiveth you receiveth me, and he that receiveth me receiveth him that sent me. *He that receiveth a prophet in the name of a prophet shall receive a prophet's rewards; and he that receiveth a righteous man shall receive a righteous man's reward. Matt. 10:40*

Doctor Ashby scheduled me for a biopsy at the Hospital and gave me instructions not to eat anything after a certain hour. The next morning my mother escorted me to the Hospital. I must confess, as rebellious and hardheaded as I was, I found myself on a bed being rolled into the elevator, begging my mom not to leave me.

I Thank God for my mother and for God giving her the ability to look beyond my faults and not give up on me.

When I regained consciousness, my mom and sister was in the room with me. My throat was dry and I felt thirsty. I asked my sister for something to drink. She innocently gave me a cup of orange soda and before I knew it, the soda and everything within me came up and out. After they cleaned me up, my doctor came in with his report. I would like to inject the fact that I also went to a specialist for a second opinion before agreeing to being admitted to the hospital for a Biopsy.

Dr. Ashby made a statement that day that helped me to realize that God was real. He said, "We opened you up and we couldn't find anything." No more cancer. I experienced great joy that day even though I had to spend the night in the hospital because I upchucked the soda. God had supernaturally healed me from cancer. No more cancer. Hallelujah! Thank you Jesus! *Bless the Lord, O my soul, and forget not all His benefits; who forgives all your iniquities, who heals all your diseases. Ps 103:3*

Jesus paid the price for our healing though the many blows He endured on his body and the innocent blood that He shed on the cross for you and me. If you are born again healing is part of your inheritance and covenant rights. It's Gods intentions for His people to prosper, be in health (good health) even as there souls prosper.

Your situation is not to hard for God, and it's not to late for God to change your outcome. Whatever you're going through right now, it's just another opportunity for God to show Himself strong on your behalf. Just trust Him. He's real and He loves you unconditionally.

Ask Him to heal you in Jesus name and believe in Him that it's done (that you are healed). God can turn your situation around that He can get the glory and you can get the victory over cancer or any other disease.

After God healed me from cancer at seventeen years old, I repented of my sins and asked Jesus Christ to come into my life and save me. And He did.

God dissolves Lumps and Growths

I'm so grateful that long suffering is a distinct character trait of God.

The lord is not slack concerning his promises, as some count slackness, but is longsuffering towards us, not willing that any should perish but that all should come to repentance. 2Peter 3:9

My cousin invited my family and I to attend church with her one Mothers Day. To my surprise, in the beginning of the Worship Service, they began to sing a song that pave the way to my much needed inner healing. I remembered it just like it was yesterday.

They sang: I love you with the love of God; I love you with the love of God. I can see in you the Glory of our king, and I love you with the love of God.

After singing it a couple of times, the Worship leader asked that we take someone by the hand and sing this song to them. As my cousin took me by my hands and began to sing to me, tears began to flow out of my eyes like someone had turned on a faucet. The words began to touch areas in my life that were previously wounded, abused and shattered.

He heals the brokenhearted and binds up their wounds. Ps 147:3

The presence of God was so strong, it was as God Himself was there saying I love you to me personally. This was my first time being in a church service where I felt the power of God so strongly. I'll never forget the love of God I experienced there. It was then that I realized it was more to being a Christian than just attending Church every now and then. Later that day I prayed the sinner's prayer but this time I committed my life to serving God. *The goodness of God leadeth thee to repentance. Romans 2:4*

During this season in my life, I discovered a lump in my left breast and the thought of possibly loosing my breast terrified me. The next Sunday I returned to the same church. They invited people to come up for prayer, so I went up to the altar for prayer at the end of the service. I asked the

Pastor to pray for me about the lump in my breast. He prayed but he didn't stop there he told me to believe that God healed me and from now on begin to thank God for healing me. He instructed me not to go by what it looked like and do not go by what I felt during my self-examinations, just have faith in God. *For we walk by faith not by sight. 2 Cor. 5:7*

That night after church, I examined myself to determine the outcome of the lump. To my surprise it was still there but I remembered and followed the instructions given by Pastor Lewis. Hear instruction and be wise, and do not disdain it. Prov. 8:33

He advised me not to go by what I felt or what I could see with my own eyes. So in spite of what my physical condition was crying out. I opened my mouth and began to proclaim that I was healed in Jesus name and I thank God for healing me.

Each time I examined myself the lump was still there, but I refused to verbalize the natural condition of my flesh. Instead I continued to say with my mouth what I was instructed to say, that I was healed in Jesus Name. *Who his own self bare our sins in his own body on the tree, that we, being dead to sins, should live unto righteousness: By whose stripes (wounds) ye were healed. 1 Peter 2:24*

Therefore I say unto you, what things soever ye desire, when ye pray, believe that ye receive them, and ye shall have them. Still walking by faith, confessing I'm healed in Jesus name but now I'm growing spiritually and attending church regularly. Every day I examined myself and made the same confessions all the way to the doctor's office. While lying on the examining table awaiting the doctor's exam, I checked for the lump, it was still there. Without reservation, I made the same confessions that I was healed in Jesus name. The doctor came in, examined my breast and asked, "What lump?" I did the exam after she did and the lump was completely gone. God did it again! I kept saying what I wanted which was healing, added faith to my daily confessions, and I received exactly what I desired. The lump was gone and without a doubt it was God that healed me. *And Jesus answering saith unto them, Have faith in God. For verily I say unto you, That whosoever shall say unto this mountain, Be thou removed, and be thou cast into the sea; and shall believe that those things which he saith shall come to pass; he shall have whatsoever he says. Mark 11:22-23*

Lumps - growths - tumors - cancer, it doesn't matter; God is able to heal you and set you free from them all. Jesus

Christ the same yesterday, today and forever. God still heals today.

It doesn't matter how long you've been sick God can deliver you from it.

It was a woman in the bible who had a spirit of infirmity eighteen years, and was bent over and could in no way raise herself up. But when Jesus saw her, He called her to Him and said to her, "Woman, you are loosed from your infirmity." And he laid His hands on her, and immediately she was made straight, and glorified God. Luke 13:11

And when Jesus was come into Peter's house, he saw his wife's mother laid, and sick of a fever. And he touched her hand, and the fever left her; and she arose, and ministered unto them. Mark 1:29

He's not a respecter of persons. He healed the woman that was bent over for eighteen years, He healed Peter's mother-in-law, He healed me and He wants to heal you. Sickness does not come from God. The thief (satan) cometh not but for to steal, and to kill, and to destroy; I (Jesus) am come that they (you) might have life, and that they might have it more abundantly.

Sickness, disease and infirmity are not considered abundant life. God wants us healed, blessed and nothing less.

Remember: Beloved, I wish above all things (pray that in all things) that thou mayest prosper and be in health, even as thy soul prospereth.

Whose report will you believe?

After the birth of my forth son, I went to the doctors office for my 6 week checkup. The doctor came in the room where I was sitting on the table after my exam. He sat down in front of me an looked me in the eyes and said, "Mrs. Forrest we see the beginning signs of cancer." As he continued to talk to me I heard another voice speaking at the same time. It was the Holy Spirit. He told me, "you can believe the doctors report concerning your health, or you can believe the word of God." He said, "the doctors report is factual, it's based on medical facts. But my word, the word of God is based on truth and the word says by His stripes (the stripes Jesus bore on his body for us) you are healed. He told me if I believed the doctors report I would have to take chemotherapy, would loose my hair and could die". Next He said, "if you believe my word, I will give you life and that more abundantly and I'll bless you on top of that." Then he asked me a question, "Whose report will you believe?"

At the end of the conversation I chose to believe the report of the Lord, which is found in the word of God. The truth. *God is not a man, that He should lie, nor the son of man, that he should repent. Has He said, and will he not make it good? Num. 23:19*

When I left the doctors office, The Holy Spirit began to give me instructions; His instructions were specific and to the point. The first thing he said was, "Do not tell people you have cancer. If you have to say anything at all, tell them the doctor said he saw cancer but you don't receive it." Then he said, "Do not share this with everybody, just your husband and those of faith that can agree in prayer with you." Last he said, "Find healing scriptures in the bible and read them out loud everyday and believe God for the manifestation."

I went home amazed at what just happened. I had an encounter with the Spirit of God right there in the doctor's office. I was sitting there facing the doctor, he was talking to me and The Holy Spirit was talking to me at the exact same time.

I remembered how God healed me at age 17 from cancer, and he later healed me from the lump on my breast. So I followed his instructions without reservation. I didn't receive the doctor's report. As a man thinketh in his heart so is he. If asked about it, my response was, "the doctor said... but I don't receive it. I believe by Jesus stripes I am healed." I only shared it with my husband. I went home opened my bible and wrote down every healing scripture I could find. Each day I read aloud the healing scriptures. So then faith comes by hearing, and by hearing the word of God. It's even more powerful when you hear yourself saying it. It will strengthen you and cause your faith to grow. The more I spoke the scriptures out of my mouth; the word of God began to get into my spirit. I went from just reading them to believing them. *My son, give attention to my words; incline your ear to my sayings. Do not let them depart from your eyes; Keep them in the midst of your heart; for they are life to those who find them, and health to all their flesh. Proverbs 4:20-22 NKJV*

Proverbs also tells us that *death and life are in the power of the tongue,* it's imperative when you need a miracle, to watch what you say. Faith filled positive words bring about positive results; doubt filled words bring about death. You can change your situation around, simply by changing your conversation and speaking words of faith out of your mouth.

Start saying, "I shall live and not die in Jesus Name." Purpose in your heart that you are going to trust and have faith in God. Began to speak the word of God over your body daily and tell yourself I am healed in Jesus name. And again expect to be healed.

God has given us the keys to the kingdom, power and authority as sons of God to bind up sickness and loose healing to flow in our bodies. *Matthews 18:18 says, "Whatever I bind on earth shall be bound in heaven and whatever I loose on earth will be loosed in heaven.* Whatever we disallow on earth shall be disallowed in heaven and whatever we allow on earth shall be allowed in heaven."

After following the instructions I was given from the Holy Spirit, He told me to start thanking God daily for healing me. So as instructed, every day I would get up and began to thank God that I was healed in Jesus Name. Every time a thought would come to my mind contrary to the word of God concerning my healing and life, I would bind it up, cast it out and began to verbally thank God for healing me all over again.

I refuse to listen to, or receive any words of doubt and unbelief, regardless of where it was coming from.

Doubt and unbelief are huge blessing blockers. The Israelites suffered unnecessary hardship, premature death, and wandered in the wilderness 40 years because of it.

It is written the just shall live by faith.

Sometimes I would be watching a healing service on television and I would feel lead to go lay my hand on the TV screen for agreement in prayer. Again I say unto you, that if two of you shall agree on earth as touching any thing that they shall ask, it shall be done for them of my Father, which is in heaven. Matt 18:19

There is power in agreement, so be careful whom you set yourself in agreement with.

If it's negative, or not of God, don't agree with it, bind it up, and disallow it.

There are great benefits in saying the scriptures out of your mouth; I quoted healing scriptures until they penetrated my spirit as truth. My mind was transformed from hearing I was healed, to knowing by His (Jesus) stripes I am healed!

A few months had past when the Holy Spirit gave me my final instructions. He told me to continue what I was doing by believing and reading the scriptures out loud and thanking Him that I was healed, but now it was time to set my doctors appointment. He wanted me to start thanking God that when

I went to the doctor, there would be no cancer in my body, because by Jesus stripes I was healed!

So I called and made a doctors appointment and I continued to follow His instruction.

Fear is the opposite of faith and cousins to doubt and unbelief. When believing God for your healing or a miracle, there's no room for either one. Choose to stay in faith.

We have to cast down arguments and every high thing that exalts itself against the knowledge of God, bringing every thought into captivity to the obedience of Christ. 2 Cor. 10:5

God is real and he's still healing today. Don't miss your miracle; hold fast to your faith, God will come through for you! Fear not, for I am with you; be not dismayed, for I am your God. I will strengthen you, yes, I will help you, *I will uphold you with My righteous right hand. Isaiah 41:10 NKJV*

After months of daily following instructions, I'm sitting in the doctor's office waiting to have a pap smear. The doctor completed his exam and I was told if there were anything abnormal, they would call me.

A couple of days went by, and I picked up the phone and called them. I asked if my test results were back, and she said, "yes everything was normal." So I asked if they checked for cancer and they said, "Yes. There was no cancer found in my body." Glory! Hallelujah! God did it again. *Bless the Lord, O my soul, and forget not all His benefits; Who forgives all your iniquities, who heals all your diseases.*

On two separate occasions in my life, God healed me of cancer. It wasn't because I was some great perfect person; it was because I dared to believe. I exercised my faith by having faith in Him, and I followed His instructions. I never took chemotherapy, and I didn't have to lose my hair; not to mention it was totally free. The only money I spent was the co-pay for my doctor's appointment. Needless to say, it was worth it and just like He healed me, He wants to heal you. You don't have to recreate the wheel. Follow the same instructions God gave me. It worked for me, and it will work for you! Try it: don't hesitate. God loves you and He wants you healed. *That it might be fulfilled which was spoken by Isaiah the prophet, saying: "He Himself took our infirmities and bore our sicknesses."*

Our Provision is Wrapped up in Our Obedience

The above statement is not just for finances: it also includes healing. Yes, it takes faith, but along with faith we have to be willing to obey Gods instructions as part of the process. *Ask, and it will be given to you; seek, and you will find; knock, and it will be opened to you. For everyone who asks receives, and he who seeks finds, and to him who knocks it will be opened. Luke 11:9-10*

On Every bottle of medicine, the instructions on how to take it, is written on the label or included in the bag, when you pick it up from the pharmacy. Most believe that as long as they follow the instructions, (while taking the medicine) they will obtain the results they desire.

God wants us healed and blessed, but we have to be willing to step out of the boat on faith, and follow His instructions in order to receive our healing without side effects or unnecessarily destroying our organs.

One day I prayed for God to heal my body from an infirmity. As I was watching a Christian television program, I heard a woman telling her testimony of how she was healed from her infirmity. She testified that she was meditating on the scripture: Surely He has borne our grief's and carried our sorrows; yet we esteemed Him stricken, smitten by God, and afflicted. *But He was wounded for our transgressions, He was bruised for our iniquities; the chastisement for our peace was upon Him, and by His stripes we are healed. Isaiah 53:4-5* She began to say, " By His stripes we are healed, and by His stripes I am healed, repeatedly until all of a sudden it was like a light came on and she realized she was healed, and the infirmity left her body. To God be the Glory!

Over the years I've learned that it's unnecessary to recreate the wheel, in other words if it worked for this precious sister it will work for me. In order to experience healing as a provision, I had to be obedient and act on what God allowed me to hear. While taking a shower, I began to meditate on the same scripture. By His stripes we are healed to by His stripes I am healed. I said the scriptures repeatedly, until all of a sudden, it happened! It was just like the sister in Christ said;

it was like the light came on, The Word of God became alive and I walked out of my shower healed from my infirmity and rejoicing in the God of my salvation.

Now it happened on another Sabbath, also that He entered the synagogue and taught; and a man was there whose right hand was withered. So the scribes and Pharisees watched Him closely, whether He would heal on the Sabbath, that they might find an accusation against Him, but he knew their thoughts, and said to the man who had the withered hand, "arise and stand here." And he arose and stood. Then Jesus said to them, I will ask you one thing; Is it lawful on the Sabbath to do good or to do evil, to save life or to destroy?" And when he had looked around at them all, He said to the man, "stretch out your hand" and he did so, and his hand was restored as whole as the other. Mark 3:1-6

Whether the act of obedience is repeating the same scripture, stretch forth your hand or have faith in God, we must be willing to do whatever He tells us to do in order to receive our healing. God honors Obedience as well as faith. *If you are willing and obedient, you shall eat the good of the land. Isa. 1:19*

The Blessing of Obedience are found in:

Deuteronomy 28:1-14

1. Now it shall come to pass, if you diligently obey the voice of the Lord your God, to observe carefully all His commandments which I command you today, that the Lord your God will set you high above all nations of the earth.
2. And all these blessings shall come upon you and overtake you, because you obey the voice of the Lord your God:
3. Blessed shall you be in the city, and blessed shall you be in the country.
4. Blessed shall be the fruit of your body, the produce of your ground and the increase of your herds, the increase of your cattle and the offspring of your flocks.
5. Blessed shall be your basket and your kneading bowl.
6. Blessed shall you be when you come in, and blessed shall you be when you go out.
7. The lord will cause your enemies who rise against you to be defeated before your face; they shall come out against you one way and flee before you seven ways;
8. The lord will command the blessing on you in your storehouses and in all to which you set your hand, and He will

bless you in the land which the Lord your God is giving you.

9. The Lord will establish you as a holy people to Himself, just as He has sworn to you, if you keep the commandments of the Lord your God and walk in His ways. Then all peoples of the earth shall see that you are called by the name of the Lord, and they shall be afraid of you.

11. And the Lord will grant you plenty of goods, in the fruit of your body, in the increase of your livestock, and in the produce of your ground, in the land of which the Lord swore to your fathers to give you.

12. The Lord will open to you His good treasure, the heavens, to give the rain to your land in its season, and to bless all the work of your hand. You shall lend to many nations, but you shall not borrow.

13. And the Lord will make you the head and not the tail; you shall be above only, and not be beneath, if you heed the commandments of the Lord your God, which I command you today, and are careful to observe them.

14. So you shall not turn aside from any of the words which I command you this day, to the right or the left, to go after other gods to serve them.

The paralyzing affects of unforgiveness

F*or you, Lord, are good, and ready to forgive, and abundant in mercy to all those who call upon you.*

Unforgiveness is like a cancer that eats away at the soul of a person. It's a stronghold that satan uses to his advantage, to stifle spiritual growth and maturity. It festers death, destruction and it paralyzes our ability to enter into the promises of God. Just like doubt, unbelief and fear it delays the manifestation of answered prayer.

The bible admonishes us to forgive our brothers that trespass against us seventy times seven times a day, and to be mindful that *whenever you stand praying, if you have anything against anyone, forgive him. That your Father in heaven may also forgive you your trespasses.* But if you do not forgive, neither will your father in heaven forgive your trespasses. It warns us: Be angry, and do not sin. Do not let the sun go down on your wrath, nor give place to the devil.

Unforgiveness causes sickness; it destroys relationships, and is the root cause of bitterness, discord and hatred towards others.

We've all been given a free will to choose right from wrong. We must choose to forgive. God forgave us for the sins and trespasses that were plaguing our lives. He expects us to be Christ like, and follow His example by forgiving others.

Jesus wasn't immune from pain, hurt or suffering. He, who was without sin, was violated, humiliated, rejected and disrespected by the people that He loved. Jesus experienced and felt every excruciating blow to his body from birth to Him laying down His life on the cross. When they placed the crown of thorns on His head it wasn't cushioned, it was real. It tore His skin, and the blood of our Savior flowed from his Head. They nailed Him to the cross and out of their ignorance they marked and blasphemed Him. Yet in spite of all that He suffered He chose to forgive. *Surely He has borne our griefs and carried our sorrows; yet we esteemed Him stricken, smitten by God, and afflicted. But He was wounded (or pierced through) for our transgressions, he was bruised (crushed) for our iniquities; the chastisement of our peace was upon him; and with his stripes (blows that cut in) we are healed.*

Why did He endure the suffering and pain? The answer is simple, for you and me. Jesus said, "As the father loved Me, *I also have loved you; abide in My love. If you keep My commandments, you will abide in my love, just as I have kept my Father's commandments and abide in His love. These things I have spoken to you, that my joy may remain in you, and that your joy may be full. This is my commandment, that you love one another as I have loved you. Greater love has no one than this, than to lay down one's life for his friends. You are My friends if you do whatever I command you. No longer do I call you servants, for a servant does not know what his master is doing, but I have called you friends, for all things that I heard from my Father I have made known to you.*"

Unforgiveness is a stronghold satan often uses as a hindrance, in the life of a believer. We have to make sure that doubt, unbelief, unforgiveness or sin isn't stopping the miraculous from being manifested on our behalf.

Healing Scriptures

And whatever you ask in My name, that I will do, that the Father may be glorified in the Son. If you ask anything in My name, I will do it. John 14:13-14 NKJV

Ask, and it will be given to you; seek, and you will find; knock, and it will be opened to you. For everyone who asks receives, and he who seeks finds, and to him who knocks it will be opened. Matt. 7:7-8 NKJV

But to you who fear my name, the Son of Righteousness shall arise with healing in His wings. Mal. 4:2b

He heals the brokenhearted and binds up their wounds. Psalms 147:3

Bless the Lord, O my soul and all that is within me, bless His holy name!
Bless the lord, O my soul, and forget not all His benefits;
Who forgives all our iniquities who heals all your diseases,
Who redeems your life from destruction who crowns you with loving kindness and tender mercies. Who satisfies your mouth with good things,
So that your youth is renewed like the eagle's.
Psalms 103:3-5

My son, give attention to my words; Incline your ear to my sayings. Do not let them depart from your eyes; keep them in the midst of your heart; for they are life to those who find them, and health to all their flesh. Prov. 4:20-22

Now this is the confidence that we have in Him, that if we ask anything according to His will, He hears us. And if we know that he hears us, whatever we ask, we know that we have the petitions that we have asked of Him. I John 5:14-15

He who did not spare His own Son, but delivered Him up for us all, how shall He not with him also freely give us all things? Rom 8:32

Fear not, for I am with you; be not dismayed, for I am your God. I will strengthen you, yes, I will help you, I will uphold you with My righteous right hand. Isaiah 41:10

And the Lord will take away from you all sickness, and will afflict you with none of the terrible diseases of Egypt which you have known, but will lay them on all those who hate you. Deut. 7:15

And said, If you diligently heed the voice of the Lord your God and do what is right in His sight, give ear to His commandment and keep all His statutes, I will put none of the diseases on you which I have brought on the Egyptians. For I am the Lord who heals you. Exodus 15:26

God is not a man, that He should lie, Nor a son of man, that He should repent, Has He said, and will He not do? Or has He spoken, and will He not make it good? Numbers 23:19

Fear not, for I am with you; be not dismayed, for I am your God. I will strengthen you, yes, I will help you, I will uphold you with My righteous right hand. Isaiah 41:10

Surely He has borne our grief's and carried our sorrows; yet we esteemed Him stricken, smitten by God, and afflicted. But He was wounded for our transgressions, He was bruised for our iniquities; the chastisement for our peace was upon Him, and by His stripes we are healed. Isaiah 53:4-5

My son, give attention to my words; incline your ear to my sayings. Do not let them depart from your eyes; Keep them in the midst of your heart; for they are life to those who find them, and health to all their flesh. Proverbs 4:20-22

For I will restore health to you and heal you of your wounds, says the Lord, because they called you an outcast saying this is Zion; "No one seeks her." Jeremiah 30:17

Bless the Lord, O my soul, and forget not all His benefits; Who forgives all your iniquities, who heals all your diseases. Psalms 103:2-3

He heals the brokenhearted and binds up their wounds. Psalm 147:3

O Lord my God, I cried out to you, and you healed me. Psalm 30:2

Many are the afflictions of the righteous, But the Lord delivers him out of them all. Psalm 34:19

That it might be fulfilled which was spoken by Isaiah the prophet, saying: "He Himself took our infirmities and bore our sicknesses" Matthew 8:17

Who Himself bore our sins in His own body on the tree, that we, having died to sins might live for righteousness-by whose stripes you were healed. 1 Peter 2:24

You shall walk in all the ways which the Lord your God has commanded you; that you may live and that it may be well with you, and that you may prolong your days in the land which you shall possess. Deuteronomy 5:33

Because you have made the Lord, who is my refuge, even the Most High, your dwelling place, No evil shall befall you, nor shall any plague come near your dwelling; for He shall give His angels charge over you, to keep you in all your ways. Psalm 91:9-11

He shall call upon me, and I will answer him; I will be with him in trouble; I will deliver him and honor him. With long life I will satisfy him, and show him my salvation. Psalm 91:15-16

For by me your days will be multiplied, and years of life will be added to you. Proverbs 9:11

But those who wait on the Lord shall renew their strength; They shall mount up with wings like eagles, They shall run and not be weary, They shall walk and not faint. Isaiah 40:31

Healings in the Bible

Peter's Mother-in-law healed

Now as soon as they had come out of the synagogue, they entered the house of Simon and Andrew, with James and John. But Simon's wife's mother lay sick with a fever, and they told him about her at once. So He came and took her by the hand and lifted her up, and immediately the fever left her, and she served them. Mark 1:29-31

Many healed after Sabbath Sunset

At evening, when the sun had set, they brought to Him all who were sick and those who were demon possessed. And the whole city was gathered together at the door. Then He healed many who were sick with various diseases, and cast out many demons; and He did not allow the demons to speak, because they knew Him. Mark 1:32-34

Jesus Forgives and Heals a Paralytic

Then they came to Him, bringing a paralytic who was carried by four men. And when they could not come near Him because of the crowd, they uncovered the roof where He was. So when they had broken through, they let down the bed on which the paralytic was lying. When Jesus saw their faith, He said to the paralytic, "Son your sins are forgiven you." Mark 2:3-5

He said to the paralytic, "I say to you, arise, take up your bed, and go to your house." Immediately he arose, took up the bed, and went out in the presence of them all, so that all were amazed and glorified God, saying, " We never saw anything like this! Mark 2:11-12

Girls restored to life and a Woman Healed

And behold, one of the rulers of the synagogue came, Jairus by name. And when he saw Him, he fell at His feet and begged Him earnestly, saying, My little daughter lies at the point of death. Come and lay Your hands on her, that she may be healed, and she will live. So Jesus went with him, and a great multitude followed Him and thronged Him.

Now a certain woman had a flow of blood for twelve years, and had suffered many things from many physicians. She had spent all that she had and was no better, but rather grew worse, when she heard about Jesus, she came behind Him in the crowd and touched His garment. For she said, If only I may touch His clothes, I shall be made well.

Immediately the fountain of her blood was dried up, and she felt in her body that she was healed of the affliction. And Jesus, immediately knowing in Himself that power had gone out of Him, turned around in the crowd and said, "Who touched My clothes?" But His disciples said to Him, "you see the multitude thronging You, and You say, "Who touched Me?" and He looked around to see her who had done this thing. But the woman, fearing and trembling, knowing what had happened to her, came and fell down before Him and told Him the whole truth. And He said to her, "Daughter, your faith has made you well. Go in peace, and be healed of your affliction." Mark 5:22-32

Verse 38-42 Then He came to the house of the ruler of the synagogue, and saw a tumult and those who wept and wailed loudly. When He came in, He said to them, "why make this commotion and weep? The child is not dead, but sleeping." and they ridiculed Him, But when He had put them all outside, He took the father and the mother of the child, and those who were with Him, and entered where the child was lying. Then He took the child by the hand, and said to her, Talitha cumi, which is translated, "Little girl, I say to you, arise." Immediately the girl arose and walked, for she was twelve years of age. And they were overcome with great amazement.

Many Touch Him and Are Made Well

When they had crossed over, they came to the land of Gennesaret and anchored there. And when they came out of the boat, immediately the people recognized Him, ran through that whole surrounding region, and began to carry about on beds those who were sick to wherever they heard

He was. Wherever He entered, into villages, cities, or the country, they laid the sick in the market please, and begged Him that they might just touch the hem of His garment. And as many as touched Him were made well. Mark 6:53-56

Jesus Heals a Deaf-Mute

Again, departing from the region of Tyre and Sidon, He came through the midst of the region of Decapolis to the Sea of Galilee. Then they brought to Him one who was deaf and had an impediment in his speech, and they begged him to put His hand on him. And He took him aside from the multitude, and put His fingers in his ears, and He spat and touched his tongue. Then looking up to heaven, He sighed, and said to him, Ephphatha, that Is, "Be opened."

Immediately his ears were opened, and the impediment of his tongue was loosed, and he spoke plainly. Then He commanded them that they should tell no one; but the more he commanded them, the more widely they proclaimed it. And they were astonished beyond measure, saying, "He has done all things well. He makes both the deaf to hear and the mute to speak." Mark 7:31-37

A Blind Man Healed at Bethsaida

Then he came to Bethsaida; and they brought a blind man to Him, and begged Him to touch him. So He took the blind man by the hand and led him out of the town. And when he had spit on his eyes and put His hands on him, He asked him if he saw anything. And he looked up and said, "I see men like trees, walking." Then He put His hands on his eyes again and made him look up. And he was restored and saw everyone clearly. Mark 8:22-26

Jesus Heals Blind Bartimaeus

Now they came to Jericho As he went out of Jericho with His disciples and a great multitude, Blind Bartimaeus, the son of Timaeus, sat by the road begging. And when he heard that it was Jesus of Nazareth, he began to cry out and say, "Jesus, Son of David, have mercy on me!" So Jesus stood still and commanded him to be called. Then they called. Then they called the blind man, saying to him, "Be of good cheer. Rise, He is calling you." And throwing aside his garment, he rose and came to Jesus. So Jesus answered and said to him, "What do you want Me to do for you?" The blind man said to Him,

" Rabboni, that I may receive my sight." Then Jesus said to him, "Go your way; your faith has made you well." and immediately he received his sight and followed Jesus on the road. Mark 10:46-52

Jesus Cleanses a Leper

And it happened when he was in a certain city, that behold, a man who was full of leprosy saw Jesus; and he fell on his face and implored Him, saying, "Lord, if You are willing, You can make me clean." Then He put out His hand and touched him, saying, "I am willing; be cleansed," Immediately the leprosy left him. And He charged him to tell no one, "But go and show yourself to the priest, and make an offering for your cleansing, as a testimony to them, just as Moses commanded." Luke 5:12-14

Jesus Heals a Great Multitude

And He came down with them and stood on a level place with a crowd of His disciples and great multitude of people from all Judea and Jerusalem, and from the seacoast of Tyre and Sidon, who came to hear Him and be healed of their diseases, as well as those who were tormented with unclean spirits. And they were healed. And the whole multitude sought to touch Him, for power went out from Him and healed them all. Luke 6:17-19

Jesus Heals a Centurion's Servant

Now when He concluded all His saying in the hearing of the people, He entered Capernaum. And a certain centurion's servant, who was dear to him, was sick and ready to die. So when he heard about Jesus, he sent elders of the Jews to Him, pleading with Him to come and heal his servant. And when they came to Jesus, they begged Him earnestly, saying that the one for whom he should do this was deserving, for he loves our nation, and has built us a synagogue." then Jesus went with them. And when He was already not far from the house, the centurion sent friends to Him, saying to Him, Lord. Do not trouble Yourself, for I am not worthy that You should enter under my roof. Therefore I did not even think myself worthy to come to You. But say the word, and my servant, will be healed.

When Jesus heard these things, He marveled at him, and turned around and said to the crowd that followed Him, "I say to you, I have not found such great faith, not even in Israel!" and those who were sent, returning to the house, found the servant well who had been sick. Luke 7:1-9

Jesus Raises the Son of the Widow of Nain

Now it happened, the day after, that he went into a city called Nain; and many of His disciples went with Him, and a large crowd. And when He came near the gate of the city, behold, a dead man was being carried out, the only son of his mother; and she was a widow. And a large crowd from the city was with her. When the Lord saw her, He had compassion on her and said to her, do not weep. Then He came and touched the open coffin, and those who carried him stood still, and He said, "Young man, I say to you, arise." So he who was dead sat up and began to speak. And He presented him to his mother. Luke 7:11-15

Conclusion

Jesus Christ the same yesterday today and forever. Your situation is not too hard for God to handle. It doesn't matter how long you've been sick, or the details of your doctor's report, God is still able to turn it around. God loves you unconditionally; He wants to heal you, just like he's healed so many that had the same condition.

Nothing is too hard for God. No matter how dead it looks or how close to death you feel. God is able to restore your health. He raised Lazarus from the dead, and without doubt, He can restore you. It's not to late; your situation is just another opportunity for God to show Himself strong on your behalf. God can, God will and God wants to heal you. Faith in God will unlock the door to receive your healing, miracle, blessing, favor and opportunities.

...But He was wounded for our transgressions, He was bruised for our iniquities; The chastisement for our peace was upon Him, and by His stripes we are healed.

Salvation Message: The Simple Truth

John 3:16 says, "For God so loved the world that He gave His only begotten Son, that whoever believes in Him should not perish but have everlasting life."

God wants us to have everlasting life. There is life after physical death. Our spirit will spend eternity in Heaven or in Hell. The bible tells us the choice is ours, because God has given us all a free will. He loves us unconditionally, even to the point that when we repent of our sins, He forgives us immediately.

To receive everlasting life, we must invite Jesus Christ into our heart to save us. It's simple, painless, but yet life changing.

Pray this simple prayer:

Dear God,

I repent of every sin that I have committed and I ask for your forgiveness in Jesus name. I ask that you come into my heart and save me, deliver me, heal me, and make my salvation real to me. I accept You today as my Lord and Savior, in Jesus name, Amen.

Glory, hallelujah! The angels in Heaven are rejoicing behind your decision for salvation.

If you prayed this prayer for the first time we would like to send you free information on what to do next, or if you need prayer, or would like to share your testimony, write or email me at: prophetesscforrest@yahoo.com. Or U.S mail:

Prophetess Cheryl D. Forrest
New Creation Ministries
P.O. Box 804,
Mathews, VA 23109.

About the Author

Prophetess Cheryl D. Forrest accepted Jesus Christ as her Savior and Lord in May 1981, and was baptized in the Holy Spirit in June, of the same year. She Co-pastors New Creation Ministries (a healing and deliverance Ministry), with her husband Apostle Steven Forrest, Sr.

She received a Bachelors Degree from Logos International College and Seminary in 1998. She was ordained as a Prophets in October 2005 and has also received several Certificates from classes she completed in Ministry, Crisis Pregnancy Counseling, Domestic Violence, Parenting, Medical and many more.

She received a mandate from God in 1981 to help people make it into the Kingdom. With God's help she's been a Director of and a part of several Evangelism teams leading many in a decision to follow Christ.

God has graciously placed an anointing on her to minister to hurting women of all ages, to see them saved, healed, delivered and set free from strongholds. He has opened doors for her to preach at several women conferences and to minister one on one and to teach Healing and Deliverance classes.

In February 2005, God opened the door and with his help she preached Women Conferences, Co-pastors and Pastor Wives Conference, a Youth Conference and spoke at a Singles meeting in Kampala, Uganda where, through God's grace many were healed, delivered and set free.

God supernaturally healed her of cancer twice (without medication) and over the years God has used her to lay hands on the sick and see them recover; Such as the lame walking, deaf ears opening, backs healed and numerous other healings have taken place.

In 1999, God used Prophetess Cheryl to start New Beginnings Alternative Home, which offered free assistance and guidance to pregnant teens and women with children.

She is a coach, trainer, advisor, instructor, spiritual midwife and mother to women of all ages and backgrounds. God uses her to offer women help and encouragement to get to their next level in God, and to birth out their dreams, vision, and ministries.

The prophet speaks what the Spirit has to say to the churches and to the nations. Prophetic operations release hope, purpose, life, warnings and guidance. Prophets are gifted to bring forth a living (rhema) word to the church.

Prayer for Healing

I thank you Heavenly Father for being Jehovah Rapha, the Lord God my healer. I also thank you for your promise in the book of John, that if we ask anything according to your will, you will hear us. And if we know that you hear us, whatever we ask, we know that we have the petitions that we have asked of you.

Heavenly Father, I ask that you heal me today, and wash me from the top of my head to the bottom of my feet, with the cleansing and healing power of the Blood of Jesus Christ. I ask that you heal my mind, body and my spirit in Jesus Name. I put my total confidence and trust in you, and I receive my healing today by faith. I thank you now that by your stripes I am healed. And I thank you for healing me today, In Jesus Name. Amen

Note:

Praise is a powerful weapon that brings God on the scene, so take this time to praise God for healing you.

Now, activate your faith, by saying out of your mouth, I receive my healing today In Jesus Name. And without doubting believe that it's done. Glory to God, Hallelujah!

My prayer for you:

In the Name of Jesus Christ, I release the power of God to come upon you right now to heal your body. I pray that your mind, body and spirit will be made totally whole. And I loose you to receive your healing from God today. Beloved, in the Name of Jesus Christ rise up and be healed.

I set myself in agreement with you, that you are healed in Jesus Name. To share your testimony, email me at: prophetesscforrest@yahoo.com

CPSIA information can be obtained
at www.ICGtesting.com
Printed in the USA
BVHW01s1800090118
504854BV00001B/19/P